Tammy Wisniewski

The Beat Generation

Edited by
Juliet Haines Mofford

*Jack Kerouac's knapsack, a symbol of the "Rucksack
Revolution" envisioned by Kerouac and Gary Snyder.
(Courtesy of the Estate of Jack and Stella Kerouac)*

Discovery Enterprises, Ltd.
Carlisle, Massachusetts

© Discovery Enterprises, Ltd., Carlisle, MA 1998

ISBN 1-57960-031-X paperback edition
Library of Congress Catalog Card Number 97-77861

10 9 8 7 6 5 4 3 2 1

Printed in the United States of America

Subject Reference Guide:

The Beat Generation
edited by Juliet Haines Mofford

Beat Generation — U. S. History

Beat Writers — Literature

Jack Kerouac — Literature

Photo Credits:

Cover art: During a break in the filming of the 1959 historic Beat film, "Pull My Daisy." Left to right: Gregory Corso (back to camera), Larry Rivers, Jack Kerouac, David Amram and Allen Ginsberg. Photo by John Cohen, courtesy of David Amram.

Title page: Photo courtesy of the Lowell Historic Preservation Commission, U. S. Department of Interior.

Page 61: Photo by Jim Higgins of the Jack Kerouac Commemorative, Eastern Canal Park, Lowell, MA; sculpture by Ben Woitena, dedicated June 25, 1988, eight polished granite columns with sandblasted excerpts from Kerouac's books.

Other photos are credited where they appear in the text.

Permissions:

Pages 20, 21, 35 and 57: Copyrights by Allen Ginsberg. Reprinted by permission of HarperCollins Publishers, Inc.

Note: All of Jack Kerouac's writings in this volume are used with permission.

Table of Contents

Rebels Against Fifties Values

by
Juliet Haines Mofford

When World War II ended, most Americans were eager for a safe haven within the family, job security, and material comforts. The government offered its returning veterans education and job training through the G. I. Bill, while Federal Housing Assistance provided housing with no down payment for young families. In the 1950s, mass-produced, prefabricated homes in suburban communities was the American dream. Commuting to a corporate job in the city became the husband's way of life, while "the little woman" remained in suburbia looking after the children.

Yet fear hovered behind this dream. Sociologists would call the fifties "The Age of Anxiety." Neighbors might be grilling hamburgers over barbecue pits but they likely had a bomb shelter dug in the backyard as well. Families of the fifties lived in the shadow of the atomic bomb. The Soviet Union had, by now, detonated a nuclear bomb so American youngsters practiced "duck 'n cover drills" in classrooms. World War II was hardly over when the country was again militarily involved, this time in Korea.

Most Americans found the sense of security from sameness, quite comforting. Nonconformity was risky at a time when most jobs required taking a Loyalty Oath and swearing that you had never been, nor would ever be, a communist. Everyone watched Senator Joseph McCarthy and the House for Un-American Activities hearings on their black and white television sets. Minorities were seldom welcome in the suburbs and those who dared to live differently, were often labeled "deviant."

This era of national prosperity was also a time of racial injustice. In 1955, a black seamstress named Rosa Parks sat in the front of a bus in Montgomery, Alabama and refused to give up her seat to a white passenger when the driver ordered her to move. The same month that Jack Kerouac's *On The Road* was published, Governor Orval Faubus defied the Supreme Court order to integrate the local high school and Little Rock, Arkansas became the first battleground of the Civil Rights struggle.

The same year that Allen Ginsberg first read *Howl*, "Rock Around the Clock" by Bill Haley & the Comets hit the top of the music charts. Parents might be shocked by that singer from Memphis with the gyrating hips, but by 1956 Elvis Presley's "Heartbreak Hotel" had sold three million copies. Rock 'n Roll, considered decadent by so many Americans at the time, had come to stay.

For some post-war Americans, particularly those among the younger generation, the rows of suburban track houses were no more than "little boxes," promising imprisonment. The monotony of suburban life with its lack of ethnic and economic diversity—not to mention donning a gray, flannel suit to commute to a corporate job—seemed absolutely stifling. Disinterested in joining the "rat race," these post World War II misfits infuriated middle-class Americans because they refused to conform to the consumer culture.

Who Were the Beats?

Centered in New York City's Greenwich Village and in San Francisco, the Beat Movement was based on the spirit of nonconformity, with disdain for material possessions and the desire for spontaneous expression and personal freedom.

Poet Allen Ginsberg divided the history of the Beat Generation into four phases.

Source: Steven Watson, "Interview with Ginsberg, April 10, 1995," *The Birth of the Beat Generation: Visionaries, Rebels, and Hipsters, 1944-1960*, New York: Pantheon Books, 1995, pp. 6-7.

1) The key writers meet and are spiritually liberated
2) The literary artifacts are written
3) The battle against censorship is waged
4) Publication followed by notoriety and renown

The Beats cannot be defined by any particular literary style or form of artistic expression. Rather, the Beats represent a band of friends, some of whom were Columbia University students at the time, who met towards the end of the Second World War. This group shared mutual literary interests and influences, a common desire for uncensored self-expression and a commitment to spiritual rather than material values. They were interested in exploring creative new horizons through literary and artistic styles, relationships, travel, and religious experiences. Some, like William de Kooning, Larry Rivers,

Franz Kline, and Jackson Pollock, were painters, and expressed this new vision through abstract expressionism. This call for choice and change took theatrical form with method actors like Marlon Brando, James Dean and others trained at Lee Strasberg's Actor's Studio in New York. Indeed, after Dean's 1955 film, *Rebel Without A Cause*, the media would dub Jack Kerouac, "the literary James Dean."

Jack Kerouac, Allen Ginsberg, and William Burroughs met in New York City in 1944 before any had been published, and formed the nucleus of the Beat movement. They were soon joined by Neal Cassady, John Clellon Holmes, Gregory Corso, and others. Traveling West, some became part of San Francisco's lively literary community. Lawrence Ferlinghetti began publishing their work and Gary Snyder shared a rich knowledge of Buddhism that enhanced their spiritual quest.

They also shared an enthusiasm for black urban culture, especially as expressed by bebop. Indeed, the Beat writers would help bring black culture into mainstream American life. Black writers and painters like Ted Joans, Bob Kaufman, and poet-playwright-political-activist LeRoi Jones (now Amiri Baraka) are considered part of the Beat movement.

Robert Creeley, John Wieners, and others who once taught at experimental Black Mountain College in North Carolina, performed and published with members of the core group. Women writers such as Diane DiPrima and Joanne Kyger, also belong to Beat literature.

Source: Bruce Cook, *The Beat Generation: The Tumultuous Fifties Movement and Its Impact On Today*, New York: Charles Scribner's Sons, 1971, pp. 9-10, 223-224.

The Beats signified something important in 1950s America: a deep hunger for individual recognition, a desire to speak frankly and honestly about things that matter, and a need for personal involvement in major undertakings.

What the Beats did was to demonstrate convincingly that poetry might be restored to its old place among the performing arts. They made it accessible. They showed that the poetry of direct utterance could be easily understood and yet still be exciting. Theirs was the kind of poetry that not only inspired but encouraged others to write… Maybe you could just put down what you felt, what you believed!

From "Beat" to "Beatnik"

The origin and meaning of the term "beat" remains a matter for debate. Supposedly, it was first used by Herbert Huncke, a Times Square hustler and occasional writer, who had picked it up from carnival cronies in Chicago. The term first appeared in print in the *New York Times*, November, 1952 in an article by John Clellon Holmes entitled "This is the Beat Generation." Holmes was another friend of the original New York group and author of *Go*, the first novel published about the Beats. He defined "Beat" as "involving a sort of nakedness of mind and soul...a feeling of being reduced to the bedrock of consciousness...poor, down and out, deadbeat, used."

Jack Kerouac gave it a more mystical meaning when he called the Beat Generation "basically a religious generation" and claimed that "Beat" meant beatitude....You feel it in a beat, in jazz—real cool jazz or a good, gutty rock number." The term "Beat" was already part of the jazz musicians' vocabulary.

A San Francisco journalist is credited with coining the word "beatnik," after the Soviet Union launched *Sputnik* into space on October 4, 1957. The reporter considered the satellite and the new writers "equally far out." Beat writers disliked the term.

"Beatniks" were ridiculed and stereotyped on television shows and in B movies as bearded losers wearing berets and black turtle-neck sweaters, and playing bongo drums. "Chicks" or "dolls" in black tights and dark glasses accompanied these "hepcats" to smoke-filled coffee houses and jazz cellars. Beatniks had their own lingo, using words like "cool," "pad," "crazy," "groovy, man!," "dig?" and "Daddy-O." To middle class Americans, the Beats seemed bent on destroying the morality of youth and represented a threat to the socioeconomic values they cherished. Indeed, the Beat movement would provide a model for the rebellious youth of the sixties.

Beat Attackers and Defenders

"Beatnik" Stereotypes

Jack Kerouac became known as "King of the Beats," (a label he detested) and the man and his work became confused with the myth in the public mind. In the section that follows, a blurb from the covers of one of Kerouac's books demonstrates how popular "beatnik" stereotypes were used to increase sales.

Source: *The Dharma Bums*, New York: New American Library/Signet Books, 1958.

The sensational bestseller about two reckless wanderers out to scale the heights of life and love…From the pagan depths of Frisco's Bohemian bars to the dizzying heights of the snow-capped Sierras, this is the story of two sensation-seeking hipsters and their jet-propelled search for experience.…Here are their 'yabyun' sexual orgies, their marathon wine-drinking binges, their wild careening mountain-climbing sprees, their sky-rocketing poetry-jazz bouts— as only Jack Kerouac, author of *On The Road*, can reveal them.

According to FBI director J. Edgar Hoover, speaking at the 1960 Republican Convention, "America's three menaces were communists, beatniks, and eggheads."

These champions of experimental literary and art forms challenged professors of English and scholarly critics, long accustomed to setting the standards of literary taste. The Beats were determined to give art and poetry back to the people and the literary establishment defended their ivory towers in a vehement war of words.

Following are some examples of these bitter attacks on Beat literature and lifestyle.

In the November 30, 1959 issue of Life Magazine, *Paul O'Neil called the Beats "The Only Rebellion Around." Excerpts from O'Neil are noted below.*

Source: Thomas Parkinson, ed., *A Casebook On the Beat*, New York: Thomas Y. Crowell, 1961, pp. 232-246.

...some of the hairiest, scrawniest, and most discontented specimens of all time: the improbable rebels of the Beat Generation, who not only refuse to sample the seeping juices of American plenty and American social advance but scorn any and all who do.

The bulk of Beat writers are undisciplined and slovenly amateurs who have deluded themselves into believing their absurdities are art simply because they have rejected the form, style, and attitudes of previous generations and have seized upon obscenity as an expression of 'total personality.' They insist that poetry, until they leapt upon the scene, was written simply for other poets and 'not for the people,' but most of them not only write for but about each other and regard the 'people' as residents of Squaresville. While bawling of individuality, scores of them mimic each other as solemnly as preschool tots in play period.

Source: Robert Brustein, "The Cult of Unthink," *Horizon*, New York: American Horizon, Inc. American Heritage Publishing Co., September, 1958, Volume 1, Number 1, pp. 38-45, 134-135.

With heaves, grunts, pigment splotches, and howls, 'cool' Beat Generation practitioners of the arts are indulging in self-expression of many sorts. Brando as Stanley Kowalski, glowering, inarticulate hero of Tennessee Williams' *A Streetcar Named Desire*, personified an entire postwar generation of troubled spirits trying to find an identity. Today we find his Kowalski wherever we look, whether in our latest literature, our poetry, our painting, our movies, our popular music, or on our city streets. In one guise or another he is the hero of the Beat Generation.

...(This) new ideal image, as Brando first gave it dramatic form and as his tribal followers from coast to coast have adopted it, is that of a man of much muscle and little mind, often surly and discontented, prepared to offer violence with little provocation. He peers out at the world from under beetling eyebrows, his right hand rests casually on his right hip; walking with a slouching, shuffling gait, he scratches himself often and almost never smiles....

Whether he throws words on a page, like the San Francisco novelist Jack Kerouac, or pigment onto a canvas like the 'action' painter Franz Kline, whether he mumbles through a movie or shimmies in the frenetic gyrations of rock-'n-roll, he is a man belligerently exalting in his own inarticulateness. He 'howls' when he has the energy, and when he doesn't, sits around 'beat' and detached....He is concerned chiefly with indulging his own feelings, glorifying his own impulses, securing his own 'cool' kicks. His most characteristic sound is a stammer or a saxophone wail; his most characteristic symbol, a blotch and a glob of paint.

He exalts in solitude and frequently speaks proudly of his 'personal vision.' Yet, while outwardly individualistic and antisocial, he is inwardly conformist. He travels in packs, writes collective manifestoes, establishes group heroes like the late movie star James Dean....

The novelists and poets now centering in San Francisco are the most striking examples of conformists masquerading as rebels. They travel together, drink together, publish together, dedicate works to each other, share the same pony-tailed girls in faded blue jeans, wear a uniform costume, and take for their collective theme the trials and tribulations of their own troubled souls....

"The Know Nothing Bohemians"

In an article entitled, "The Know-Nothing Bohemians," Norman Podhoretz presented the Beats as delinquents out to destroy American literature and moral values.

Source: Norman Podhoretz, *Partisan Review*, Vol. XXV, Number 3, Spring, 1958, pp. 305-311, 313-316, 318.

The spirit of hipsterism and the Beat Generation strikes me as the same spirit which animates the young savages in leather jackets who have been running amok in the last few years with their switch blades and zip guns...what juvenile delinquency is to life, the San Francisco writers are to literature...the Beats represent a conspiracy to replace civilization with the world of the adolescent street gangs.

The Beat Defenders

This ongoing controversy served to increase their book sales and the Beats did have some able defenders.

Source: Watson, *op. cit.*, pp. 258-259.

Author and social critic Norman Mailer wrote that "The beatnik is the torch bearer of those all-but-lost values of freedom, self-expression, and equality."

Speaking at Brandeis University's Forum "Is There a Beat Generation?" on November 6, 1958, Jack Kerouac said, "Woe unto those who don't realize that America must, will, is, changing now, for the better I think....Woe unto those who would spit on the Beat Generation—the wind will blow it back."

Source: Dennis McNally, *Desolate Angel. Jack Kerouac, the Beat Generation, and America*, New York: Random House, 1979, p. 247.

In an interview by the *Saturday Review of Literature*, September 28, 1957, Kerouac enthusiastically declared, "We love everything, Billy Graham, the Big Ten, rock and roll, Zen, apple pie, Eisenhower—we dig it all. We're the vanguard of the new religion. We're basically a religious generation."

Jack Kerouac
(1922-1969)

Jack Kerouac,
c. 1965 by Jerry Bauer

"The Great Rememberer"

Source: Jack Kerouac, *Lonesome Traveler*, New York: McGraw Hill; Grove Press, 1960, Author's Introduction.

Had beautiful childhood, my father a printer in Lowell, Mass., roamed fields and riverbanks day and night, wrote little novels in my room, first novel written at age 11, also kept extensive diaries and 'newspapers' covering my own-invented horseracing and base-ball and football worlds (as recorded in novel *Doctor Sax*). —Had good early education from Jesuit brothers at St. Joseph's Parochial School in Lowell making me jump sixth grade in public school.... Decided to become a writer at age 17 under influence of Sebastian Sampas, local young poet who later died on Anzio beach head; read the life of Jack London at 18 and decided to also be an adventurer, a lonesome traveler; early literary influences Saroyan and Hemingway; later Wolfe (after I had broken leg in Freshman foot-ball at Columbia read Tom Wolfe and roamed his New York on crutches). —Influenced by older brother Gerard Kerouac who died at age 9 in 1926 when I was 4, was great painter and drawer in childhood (he was) — (also said to be a saint by the nuns) — (recorded in forthcoming novel *Visions of Gerard*)....Mother still living, I live with her a kind of monastic life that has enabled me to write as much as I did. —But also wrote on the road, as hobo, railroader, Mexican exile, Europe travel....

First formal novel *The Town and the City* written in tradition of long work and revision, from 1946 to 1948, three years, published by Harcourt Brace in 1950. —Then discovered 'spontaneous' prose and wrote, say, *The Subterraneans* in 3 nights — wrote *On the Road* in 3 weeks —

Read and studied alone all my life....Had own mind — Am known as 'madman bum and angel' with 'naked endless head' of 'prose.' —Also a verse poet, *Mexico City Blues* (1959). —Always considered writing my duty on earth. Also the preachment of universal kindness, which hysterical critics have failed to notice beneath frenetic activity of my true-story novels about the 'beat' generation. —Am actually not 'beat' but strange solitary Catholic mystic....

Final plans: hermitage in the woods, quiet writing of old age, mellow hopes of Paradise (which comes to everybody anyway).

Jack could not recall when he did not wish to be a writer, recording all that he observed and experienced in a series of narrative novels. However, he received no encouragement from his father.

Source: McNally, *op. cit.*, p. 15.

Leo Kerouac told his teenage son to "Forget this writing stuff. It'll never pay. You're such a good student. Sure, you'll go to college, get a job. Stop dreaming!"

Father Morissette, a French-Canadian priest at Jack's Catholic parish at Lowell, was more supportive. "Jack came to me when he was about sixteen and told me he wanted to be a writer but he was afraid the other kids would laugh at him and call him a sissy. 'I've got something to tell the world, and I'm going to write books,' Kerouac told the priest.

I told him he wouldn't get rich writing books but Jack said he didn't care. His family was poor but he was a good athlete so I advised him to get a scholarship and go to college."

Saturday's Hero

When Kerouac was a teenager, his father ran a gym, managed wrestling matches and promoted his son's sports career. Jack ran track, sprinting and hurdling through his senior year, running twice at the Boston Garden and becoming Lowell High's leading point-scorer. His pals nicknamed him "Zagg" for his speed and running style.

Kerouac failed to make the varsity football team his sophomore year at Lowell High School in 1937. He tried out again, but only made junior varsity and never got to play in a game because the coach considered him too small. Then, in the first varsity game of the 1938 season, Jack was put in as substitute halfback for an injured player.

Source: *Lowell Sun*, October 2, 1937.

Kerouac seems to be well on the way to becoming an excellent ball carrier...knifing for a four-yard score....Young Kerouac has the legs and the style. He looks like a football player. The sportswriter called him *Speed-king* and 'one of the fastest school boy backs in the state.'

Kerouac scored the final touchdown to win the 1938 Thanksgiving Day football game against the team from the neighboring mill town, Lawrence and became a local hero.

As his priest predicted, Kerouac was wooed by the college coaches. He received an offer from Boston College, but decided on Columbia University. Coach Lou Little sent Jack to Horace Mann Prep School for a year, where his gridiron glory was noted by New York Herald Tribune *sportswriters: "The visiting squad formed a vague background for the brilliant running of Kerouac."*

When Kerouac limped off the field early in his first season at Columbia, Coach Little ordered him to "run it off." By the next game, the pain from his hairline fracture made it impossible to play, and he explored New York on crutches.

Source: Jack Kerouac, "Interview with Al Aronowitz," *New York Post*, March 10, 1959.

I was just sitting in my dorm room and it was snowing, and it was time to go out to scrimmage. Time to go out in the snow and the mud and bang yourself around. And then suddenly, on the radio it started — Beethoven! I said, 'I'm going to be an artist. I'm not going to be a football player.' That's the night I didn't go to scrimmage. And I never went back to football, see?

The Car in Fifties Culture

"See the U. S. A. in your Chevrolet," Dinah Shore sang on the television screen. The open road or what Kerouac called "the ragged promised land, the fantastic end of America," had long held the promise of romance and adventure for Americans. In the fifties however, automobiles became symbols of the nation's material progress. Tail-fins, the bigger—the better, were status symbols, and the latest models were affordable through "easy credit" loans. A second car was now deemed a necessity for families who lived in the suburbs.

With the Federal Highway Act of 1956, Congress authorized the construction of 40,000 miles of new interstate highways that would forever change the American landscape. Thus, On The Road *can be read as nostalgia for the country's loss of unique local vistas. The first Holiday Inn opened in 1952 and Ray Kroc opened America's first "McDonald's" in Des Plaines, Illinois in 1955. The fifties are remembered for drive-in movie theaters, car-hops serving fast food at car windows, and teenage boys tinkering with their own "hot-rods." Yet the author who chronicled what is arguably the most famous cross-country automobile trip in American literature, never owned a car nor had a driver's license.*

"I'll have seen 41 states in all," Kerouac wrote his sister on September 25, 1947. "Is that enough for an American novelist?"

Source: Neal Cassady as "Dean Moriarty" in *On The Road*. Quoted by Watson, *op. cit.*, pp. 105, 98.

...Cassady suggested that he and Jack go "into action as one." On December 15, 1948, Jack heard the mad Western's excited voice over the phone. "Yes, yes, it's Neal, you see…I've got a '49 Hudson." Cassady planned to head East to pick up his buddy and then, head back West. Neal soon arrived at the Rocky Mount, North Carolina home of Jack's sister, with his ex-wife LuAnne Henderson and friend, Al Hinkle to pick him up in a brand-new, mud-spattered, maroon Hudson….On January 28, 1949, they left New York City to begin the trip that would be later fictionalized in *On The Road*.

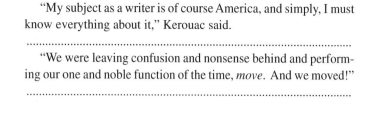

"My subject as a writer is of course America, and simply, I must know everything about it," Kerouac said.

....

"We were leaving confusion and nonsense behind and performing our one and noble function of the time, *move*. And we moved!"

....

Source: Jack Kerouac, *Visions of Cody*, New York: McGraw Hill Book Company, 1972, 1974, pp. 71-72.

The roads that Cody Pomeray knew in the West and that I rode with him later were all those tremendously frightening two-lane bumpy roads with those ditches on both sides, that poor fence, that rangefence next, maybe a sad cut of earth, a hair head of grass on a lump of sand, then endless range leading to mountains that belong to other states sometimes — but that road always seems destined to bounce you in the ditch because it humps over each way and the feeling is of the car rolling on a side angle, inclined to a ditch, a bump in the road will bounce it in — as a consequence of this western roads are lonelier to ride than any....

Neal Cassady
(1926-1968)

"A Young Gene Autry"

"A young Gene Autry — trim, thin hipped, blue-eyed with a real Oklahoma accent — a side-burned hero of the snowy West."

— Kerouac

Dean Moriarty and Cody Pomeray were Kerouac's names for Neal Cassady. With his restless energy, independent spirit and charisma, he represented the free spirit that his friends wished they could be. Cassady had grown up on skid row in the occasional care of an alcoholic father and had learned to survive by wit and charm, even if that meant spending time in jail for stealing cars or being married to more than one woman at a time. An autodidact and reported to be a gifted, if undisciplined writer, Neal was a voracious reader who could hold his own in any intellectual conversation. In the excerpts that follow, Kerouac describes his friend.

Source: Kerouac, *Visions of Cody*, *op. cit.*, pp. 48-49.

Have you ever seen anyone like Cody Pomeray? —say on a street corner on a winter night in Chicago, or better, Fargo, any mighty cold town, a young guy with a bony face that looks like it's been pressed against iron bars to get that dogged rocky look of suffering, perseverance, finally when you look closest, happy prim self-belief, with Western side-burns and big blue flirtatious eyes of an old maid and fluttering lashes; the small and muscular kind of fellow wearing usually a leather jacket and if it's a suit it's with a vest so he can prop his thick busy thumbs in place and smile the smile of his grandfathers; who walks as fast as he can go on the balls of his feet, talking excitedly and gesticulating poor pitiful kid actually just out of reform school with no money, no mother, and if you saw him dead on the sidewalk with a cop standing over him you'd walk on in a hurry, in silence. Oh life, who is that?…

Allen Ginsberg
(1926-1997)

"Dharma Lion"

Allen Ginsberg grew up in Paterson, New Jersey, where his father taught English at the public high school and wrote poetry. His mother's mental illness and eventual commitment to an institution had a profound impact upon his life and work. He received a scholarship from the Young Men's Hebrew Association to attend Columbia University and was a student when he met Jack Kerouac and others, determined to develop a new literary vision that was not being addressed by his professors. Ginsberg's writing was heavily influenced by Kerouac's "spontaneous prose" and throughout his career, In the following lines, Ginsberg lists some reasons for writing poetry.

Source: Allen Ginsberg, "Improvisation in Beijing," *Collected Poems, 1947-1980*, New York: HarperCollins, 1984, p. xiii.

I write poetry because the English word Inspiration comes from Latin *Spiritus*, breath, I want to breathe freely.

I write poetry because Walt Whitman gave world permission to speak with candor.

I write poetry because Walt Whitman opened up poetry's verse-line for unobstructed breath...

I write poetry because Ezra Pound pointed young Western poets to look at Chinese writing word pictures.

I write poetry because W. C. Williams living in Rutherford wrote New Jerseyesque 'I kick yuh eye,' asking, how measure that in iambic pentameter?

I write poetry because my father was poet my mother from Russia spoke Communist, died in a mad house.

I write poetry because young friend Gary Snyder sat to look at his thoughts as part of external phenomenal world just like a 1984 conference table.

I write poetry because I suffer, born to die, kidneystones and high
  blood pressure, everybody suffers.

I write poetry because I suffer confusion not knowing what other
  people think.

I write because poetry can reveal my thoughts, cure my paranoia
  also other people's paranoia.

I write poetry because my mind wanders subject to sex politics
  Buddhadharma meditation.

I write poetry to make accurate picture my own mind....

Ginsberg viewed the poet's role in society not only as observer, but as prophet and spokesman. He received the National Book award in 1974 and was elected to the American Academy of Arts and Letters. Familiar on the college lecture circuit, Ginsberg taught at Brooklyn College and was co-founder of the Jack Kerouac School of Disembodied Poetics at Naropa Institute in Boulder, Colorado.

Much of Ginsberg's earlier work echoes other poets he admired such as the 18th century English writer, William Blake; the poet-pediatrician from Ginsberg's hometown, William Carlos Williams; and Walt Whitman. In the following excerpt from his verses, Ginsberg addresses the author of "Leaves of Grass."

Source: Allen Ginsberg, *Howl and Other Poems*, San Francisco, California: City Lights, Pocket Poets Series: Number Four. pp. 23-24. (Allen Ginsberg Trust)

A Supermarket in California

What thoughts I have of you tonight, Walt
Whitman, for I walked down the sidestreets under the
trees with a headache self-conscious looking at the full
moon.

In my hungry fatigue, and shopping for images,
I went into the neon fruit supermarket, dreaming of
your enumerations!

What peaches and what penumbras! Whole
families shopping at night! Aisles full of husbands!
Wives in the avocados, babies in the tomatoes!...

The San Francisco Renaissance

The Six Gallery Reading

Allen Ginsberg arrived in San Francisco in 1954 with a letter of introduction from his mentor, William Carlos Williams, to the poet and critic Kenneth Rexroth, who ran a literary salon. Ginsberg got a job in market research and planned to attend graduate school at Berkeley. During the homophobic fifties, Ginsberg had experienced several heterosexual relationships but, with a psychologist's help, was finally able to feel comfortable with his homosexuality. Soon after moving in with Peter Orlovsky, who would be his companion for the next thirty years, Ginsberg was asked to arrange an event for a painter who had just opened an artists' cooperative in a former auto repair shop and wanted to get "Six Gallery" off to a lively start. Ginsberg mailed out mimeographed post cards, inviting several hundred people to a poetry reading on October 13, 1955.

Source: Cook, *op. cit.*, pp. 54-64.

6 poets at 6 Gallery. Philip Lamantia reading mss. of late John Hoffman — Mike McClure, Allen Ginsberg, Gary Snyder & Phil Whalen — all sharp new straightforward writing — remarkable collection of angels on one stage reading their poetry. No charge, small collection for wine and postcards. Charming event.

Kenneth Rexroth, M. C.

Michael McClure

At twenty-three, McClure was the youngest to read that night at Six Gallery. The following poem which he shared was written in protest of the recent killing of whales by NATO troops. The poet envisioned this recent slaughter as horrible and bloody as scenes depicted by the Spanish artist, Goya's "Horrors of War." In 1972, McClure joined Gary Snyder in lobbying on behalf of the endangered species of whales before the United Nations Environmental Conference. McClure continues to write poetry, plays and novels and to run workshops for writers. As a performance-poet, he frequently appears with Ray Manzarek, formerly the keyboardist for "The Doors."

Source: Ann Charters, ed., *The Portable Beat Reader*, New York: Viking Penguin, 1992, pp. 285-286.

For the Death of 100 Whales

Hung midsea
Like a boat mid-air
The Liners boiled their pastures:
The Liners of flesh,
The Arctic steamers.

Brains the size of a football
Mouths the size of a door.
The sleek wolves
Mowers and reapers of sea kine.
THE GIANT TADPOLES
(Meat their algae)
Lept
Like sheep or children
Shot from the sea's bore.

Turned and twisted
(Goya!!)
Flung blood and sperm.
Incense.
Gnashed at their tails and brothers,
Curses Christ of mammals,
Snapped at the sun,
Ran for the sea's floor.
Goya! Goya!...
No angels dance those bridges.
OH GUN! OH BOW!
There are no churches in the waves,
No holiness,
No passages or crossings
From the beasts' wet shore.

Allen Ginsberg

In the section that follows, Ginsberg describes the night he first read Howl, *a poem he considered too personal to ever get published.*

Source: Jane Kramer, *Allen Ginsberg in America*, New York: Random House, 1968, 1969, p. 48.

I gave a very wild, funny, tearful reading of the first part of *Howl*. Like I really felt shame and power reading it, and every time I'd finish a long line Kerouac would shout, 'Yeah!' or 'So there!...which added a kind of extra note of bop humor to the whole thing. It was like a jam session, and I was very astounded because *Howl* was a big, long poem and yet everybody seemed to understand and at the same time to sympathize with it. Like it was the end of the McCarthy scene, and here I was talking about super-Communist pamphlets on Union Square and the national Golgotha and the Fascists and all the things that turned out to be implicit in a sort of social community revolution that was actually going on. The evening ended up with everybody absolutely radiant and happy....It was an *ideal* evening, and I felt so proud and pleased and happy with the sense of 'at last a community'...

Following are some lines from Allen Ginsberg's long poem of protest that begins "I saw the best minds of my generation destroyed by madness, starving hysterical naked..."

Source: *Ibid*.

...angel headed hipsters burning for the ancient heavenly
connection to the starry dynamo in the machinery of night,
who poverty and tatters and hollow-eyed and high sat up
smoking in the supernatural darkness of cold-water flats
floating across the tops of cities contemplating jazz...
....
who talked continuously seventy hours from park to pad to bar
     to Bellevue to museum to the Brooklyn Bridge,
a lost battalion of platonic conversationalists jumping down the
     stoops off fire escapes off windowsills off Empire State
     out of the moon...

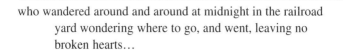

who wandered around and around at midnight in the railroad
yard wondering where to go, and went, leaving no
broken hearts...

who wept at the romance of the streets with their pushcarts full
of onions and bad music,

who sat in boxes breathing in the darkness under the bridge,
and rose up to build harpsichords in their lofts,

who coughed on the sixth floor of Harlem crowned with flame
under the tubercular sky surrounded by orange crates of
theology,

who scribbled all night rocking and rolling over lofty
incantations which in the yellow morning were stanzas
of giberish...

Source: Watson. *op. cit.*, p. 187.

In *Scratching the Beat Surface*, (San Francisco: North Point
Press, 1982), Michael McClure recalled the Six Gallery reading...

"So when Ginsberg drew the line with *Howl* we had to decide
whether our toe was on the line too. We had gone beyond a point of
no return, and we were ready for it. None of us wanted to go back
to the gray, chill, militaristic silence, to the intellectual void—to
the land without poetry—to the spiritual drabness. We wanted to
make it new and we wanted to invent it and the process of it as we
went into it. We wanted voice and we wanted vision."

*Kerouac congratulated Ginsberg and told him that his poem would make
him famous in San Francisco. Kenneth Rexroth predicted* Howl *was going to
make Allen famous from bridge to bridge. Gary Snyder described it as "a
curious kind of turning point in American poetry." Lawrence Ferlinghetti
sent Ginsberg a telegram repeating the note Emerson wrote Whitman after
reading "Leaves of Grass": "I greet you at the beginning of a great career!
When do I get the manuscript?"*

Horn on Howl

Howl was first printed in England for City Lights Press in October, 1956 and copies of its second edition were seized in San Francisco by U. S. Customs in March of 1957. The city district attorney refused to censor it but local police arrested Lawrence Ferlinghetti and his manager at their City Lights Bookstore on charges of printing and selling obscene literature. The American Civil Liberties Union defended it in court and on October 4, 1957, Howl *was vindicated by Judge Clayton W. Horn, who wrote the following, regarding his decision.*

Source: Gene Feldman & Max Gartenberg, editors, *The Beat Generation and The Angry Young Men*, New York: The Citadel Press, 1958; Dell Publishing Company, 1959, p. 182.

Life is not encased in one formula whereby everyone acts the same or conforms to a particular pattern. No two persons think alike. We are all made from the same mould, but in different patterns. Would there be any freedom of press or speech if one must reduce his vocabulary to vapid innocuous euphemism? An author should be real in treating his subject and be allowed to express his thoughts and ideas in his own words.

Ferlinghetti on Censorship

In the following selection, poet-publisher Ferlinghetti explains his point of view regarding this censorship case.

Source: Lawrence Ferlinghetti, "Horn On Howl," *Evergreen Review*, I, 4 (copyright, 1958), pp. 145-158. Reprinted Thomas Parkinson, editor, *A Casebook on the Beat*, New York: Thomas Y. Crowell Co., 1961, 1967, pp. 125-135. (Used by permission of Grove/Atlantic, Inc.)

Fahrenheit 451, the temperature at which books burn, has finally been determined not to be the prevailing temperature at San Francisco, though the police still would be all too happy to make it hot for you. On October 3 last (1957), Judge Clayton Horn of Municipal Court brought in a 39-page opinion finding Shigeyoshi Murao and myself not guilty of publishing or selling obscene writings, to wit Allen Ginsberg's *Howl and Other Poems....* Thus ended one of the most irresponsible and callous police actions to be perpetrated west of the Rockies, not counting the treatment accorded Indians and Japanese.

When William Carlos Williams in his 'Introduction' to *Howl*, said that Ginsberg had come up with 'an arresting poem' he hardly knew what he was saying.... Part of a second printing was stopped by Customs on March 25, 1957.... In defense of *Howl* I said I thought it to be 'the most significant single long poem to be published in this country since World War II, perhaps since T. S. Eliot's Four Quartets....'

On May 29 Customs released the books it had been holding, since the United States Attorney at San Francisco refused to institute condemnation proceedings against *Howl*.

Then the police took over and arrested us.... I found myself being booked and fingerprinted in San Francisco's Hall of Justice. The city jail occupies the upper floors of it, and a charming sight it is, a picturesque return to the early Middle Ages. And my enforced tour of it was a dandy way for the city officially to recognize the flowering of poetry in San Francisco. As one paper reported, "The Cops Don't Allow No Renaissance Here."

The American Civil Liberties Union posted bail.... The critical support for *Howl* (or the protest against censorship on principle) was enormous. Here is some of what some said:

> Henry Rago, editor of *Poetry* (Chicago). "...I wish only to say that the book is a thoroughly serious work of literary art.... I would be unworthy of the tradition of this magazine or simply of my place as a poet in the republic of letters, if I did not speak for the right of this book to free circulation, and against this affront not only to Allen Ginsberg and his publishers, but to the possibilities of the art of poetry in America."

....

> Counsel Bendich's argument: "The first amendment to the Constitution of the United States protecting the fundamental freedoms of speech and press prohibits the suppression of literature by the application of obscenity formulae

unless the trial court first determines that the literature in question is utterly without social importance. (Roth v. U. S.) ... all of the experts for the defense identified the main theme of *Howl* as social criticism. And the prosecution concedes that it does not understand the work, much less what its dominant theme is."

Judge Horn agreed, in his opinion: "I do not believe that *Howl* is without even 'the slightest redeeming social importance. The first part of *Howl* presents a picture of a nightmare world; the second part is an indictment of those elements in modern society destructive of the best qualities of human nature; such elements are predominantly identified as materialism, conformity, and mechanization leading toward war. The third part presents a picture of an individual who is a specific representation of what the author conceives a general condition."...

On The Road

A speed typist at 120 words per minute, Kerouac wrote the principal draft of On The Road *in three weeks on a single, 100-foot long roll of teletype paper, in run-on sentences, without paragraphs or periods, the narrative broken only by dashes. Although he wrote it years earlier, he was unable to get it published until 1957, a few months after the vindication of* Howl *in court. After severe editorial cutting on his first book,* The Town and the City, *Kerouac was determined to keep* On The Road *as he wished it to be read.*

Joyce Glassman (Johnson) grew up in New York, attended Barnard College and worked for a literary agent. She was Kerouac's girlfriend when On The Road *was finally published. In her award-winning memoir of several years spent with its author, she describes Kerouac's final moments between obscurity and fame. Of course, Jack's friends all knew he had written ten books since the one that chronicled his travels with Neal Cassady a decade before.*

Source: Joyce Johnson, *Minor Characters,* Boston, MA: Houghton Mifflin, 1983. Reprint NY: Pocket Books, Washington Square Press (Division of Simon & Schuster), pp.194-195. (To be reissued by Penguin Books, Fall 1999.)

There was a news stand at Sixty-sixth Street and Broadway right at the entrance to the subway. Just before midnight we woke up and threw on our clothes in the dark and walked down there.... According to Viking Press, there was going to be a review. "Maybe it'll be terrific. Who knows?" I said. Jack said he was doubtful.

We saw the papers come off the truck. The old man at the stand cut the brown cord with a knife and we bought the one on the top of the pile and stood under a street lamp turning pages until we found "Books of the Times." I felt dizzy reading Millstein's first paragraph—like going up on a Ferris wheel too quickly and dangling out over space, laughing and gasping at the same time. Jack was silent. After he'd read the whole thing, he said,."It's good, isn't it?" "Yes," I said. "It's very, very good."

We walked to Donnelly's and spread the paper out on the bar and read the review together, line by line, two or three more times, like students poring over a difficult text for which they sense they're going to be held responsible....

It was all very thrilling—but frightening, too. I'd read lots of reviews in my two years in publishing: None of them made pronouncements like this about history. What would history demand of Jack? What would a generation expect of its avatar? I remember wishing Allen (Ginsberg) was around to make sense of all this, instead of being in Paris.

Jack kept shaking his head. He didn't look happy, exactly, but strangely puzzled, as if he couldn't figure out why he wasn't happier than he was.

We returned to the apartment to go back to sleep. Jack lay down obscure for the last time in his life. The ringing phone woke him the next morning and he was famous.

Excerpts from the New York Times *review follow.*

Source: Gilbert Millstein, "Books of The Times," *New York Times*, Thursday, September 5, 1957.

'ON THE ROAD' is the second novel by Jack Kerouac, and its publication is a historic occasion in so far as the exposure of an authentic work of art is of any great moment in an age in which the attention is fragmented and the sensibilities are blunted by the superlatives of fashion (multiplied a millionfold by the speed and pound of communications.)

...It is possible that (the book) will be condescended to by, or make uneasy the neo-academicians and the "official" avant-garde critics, and that it will be dealt with superficially elsewhere as merely "absorbing" or "intriguing" or "picaresque" or any of a dozen convenient banalities, not excluding "off-beat." But the fact is that "On the Road" is the most beautifully executed, the clearest and the most important utterance yet made by the generation Kerouac himself names years ago as "beat," and whose principal avatar he is.

Just as more than any other novel of the Twenties, "The Sun Also Rises" came to be regarded as the testament of the "Lost Generation," so it seems certain that "One the Road" will come to be known as that of the "Beat Generation." There is otherwise, no similarity between the two; technically and philosophically, Hemingway and Kerouac are, at the very least, a depression and a world war apart.

....

Much has been made of the phenomenon that a good deal of the writing, the poetry and the painting of this generation (to say nothing of its deep interest in modern jazz) has emerged in the so-called "San Francisco Renaissance," which, while true, is irrelevant. It cannot be localized....

....

The "Beat Generation" was born disillusioned; it takes for granted the imminence of war, the barrenness of politics and the hostility of the rest of society. It is not even impressed by...material well-being....

....

That is the meaning of On the Road? What does its narrator, Sal Paradise, say? "* * * The only people for me are the mad ones, the ones who are mad to live, mad to talk, mad to be saved, desirous of everything at the same time, the ones who never yawn or say a commonplace thing, but burn, burn, burn like fabulous yellow roman candles * * *"

....

There are sections of "On the Road" in which the writing is of a beauty almost breathtaking. There is a description of a cross-country automobile ride fully the equal for example, of the train ride told by Thomas Wolfe in "Of Time and the River." There are the details of a trip to Mexico...that are by turns, awesome, tender, and funny. And finally, there is some writing on jazz that has never been equaled in American fiction, either for insight, style or technical virtuosity. "On the Road" is a major novel.

Jack Kerouac was an overnight sensation. In spite of harsh attacks from many critics and conservative scholars in the establishment, the book remained on the Best Seller List five weeks and was being bought and read by everyone. Academia generally believed that anyone this popular with the public could not possibly have written anything worthwhile.

The media cashed in on Kerouac's success with talk shows and magazine profiles. Jack declined an offer from CBS to write and appear in a television series based on the book. This show became "Route 66" and ran for four seasons, with Kerouac look-alike, George Maharis, sharing the lead with Martin Milner and driving a Corvette cross-country.

Source: Cook, *op. cit.*, p. 82.

As soon as the great publicity machine began to grind away, he found his life was not his own. As Kerouac tells it in *Big Sur*: "...I've been driven mad for three years by endless telegrams, phone calls, requests, mail, visitors, reporters, snoopers (a big voice saying in my basement window as I prepare to write a story: —ARE YOU BUSY?) or the time the reporter ran upstairs to my bedroom as I sat there in my pajamas trying to write down a dream—Teenagers jumping the six-foot fence I had built around my yard for privacy—Parties with bottles yelling at my study window 'Come on out and get drunk, all work and no play makes Jack a dull boy!'"

Kerouac's "Spontaneous Prose"

Those who knew Kerouac admired his self-discipline as a writer. According to Allen Ginsberg, "Jack always had pen and paper, as well as a five-cent spiral notepad in the pocket of his shirt. He constantly collected and processed information which he considered his job as a writer." William Burroughs said, "Jack was writing all the time. Writing was the only thing Jack thought about. He never wanted to be anything else."

Kerouac's unique style represented "undisturbed flow from the mind of personal secret ideas—the words blowing like jazz music...." Kerouac had invented a new writing style, which he believed had "intuitive honesty." He boasted that he never revised: "first word, best word."

William Burroughs and Allen Ginsberg asked Kerouac to write down his writing method which Kerouac later modified for publication. The following is Kerouac's "List of Essentials."

Source: Jack Kerouac, "Belief and Technique for Modern Prose," *Evergreen Review*, Vol. 2, No. 8 (Spring, 1959). Reprinted: Donal Allen, editor, *Good Blonde and Others* by Jack Kerouac, San Francisco, California: Grey Fox Press, 1993, pp. 72-73.

"List of Essentials"

1. Scribbled secret notebooks and wild typewritten pages, for yr own joy
2. Submissive to everything, open, listening
3. Be in love with yr life every detail of it
4. Something that you feel will find its own form
5. Be crazy dumbsaint of the mind
6. Blow as deep as you want to blow
7. Write what you want bottomless from bottom of the mind
8. The unspeakable visions of the individual
9. No time for poetry but exactly what is
10. Visionary tics shivering in the chest
11. In tranced fixation dreaming upon object before you.
12. Remove literary grammatical and syntactical inhibition
13. Like Proust be old teahead of time
14. Telling the true story of the world in interior monolog
15. The jewel center of interest is the eye within the eye
16. Write in recollection and amazement for yourself
17. Work from pithy middle eye out, swimming in language sea
18. Accept loss forever
19. Believe in the holy contour of life
20. Struggle to sketch the flow that already exists intact in mind
21. Don't think of words when you stop but to see picture better
22. Keep track of every day the date emblazoned in yr morning
23. No fear or shame in the dignity of yr experience, language & knowledge
24. Write for the world to read and see yr exact pictures of it
25. Bookmovie is the movie in words, the visual American form
26. In Praise of Character in the Bleak inhuman loneliness
27. Composing wild, undisciplined pure, coming in from under, crazier the better
28. You're a Genius all the time
29. Writer-Director of Earthly Movies sponsored & Angeled in Heaven

William Seward Burroughs
(1914-1997)

Born in 1914 in St. Louis, the grandson of the inventor of the adding machine and founder of the business machine empire, Burroughs graduated from Harvard University in 1936 and pursued graduate studies in cultural anthropology, then attended medical school in Vienna. Ginsberg met William Burroughs in 1943 and the following year, Burroughs also became Kerouac's mentor. He provided them with book lists that included works by Dostoevsky, Shakespeare, Coleridge, DeQuincy, Flaubert, Baudelaire, Rimbaud, James Joyce, Joseph Conrad, Franz Kafka, Graham Greene and Raymond Chandler. To these younger men, Burroughs seemed "the most intelligent man in the world."

Source: Cook, *op. cit.*, p. 173.

Considered by most critics to be an 'iconoclastic novelist representative of the counterculture' Burroughs considered himself a realist.... "There is only one thing a writer can write about. *What is in front of his senses at the moment of writing*...I am a recording instrument...I do not presume to impose 'story' 'plot' 'continuity' ... Insofar as I succeed in *Direct* recording of certain areas of psychic process I may have limited function. I am not an entertainer."

Source: *New York Times*, "William S. Burroughs, the Beat Writer Who Distilled His Raw Nightmare Life, Dies at 83," August 4, 1997, p. D11.

Although his family legacy provided a trust fund, Burroughs worked as a bartender, factory-hand, private detective, and insect exterminator. He lived in New Orleans, Tangiers, Paris, London, and Mexico, where over the intervening years, he was visited by Kerouac, Ginsberg, Corso, and others in the movement. Jack Kerouac wrote *Doctor Sax* and most of *Mexico City Blues* while staying with Burroughs in Mexico.

Burroughs was also a serious photographer and painter, although for the fifteen years he was addicted to heroin, he claimed he "did absolutely nothing".... "the Ugly Spirit maneuvered me into a life-long struggle, in which I have had no choice but to write my way out.... My entire life has been a struggle to resist the dark force."

Naked Lunch

"A frozen moment when everyone sees what is on the end of every fork."

— Kerouac

Jack Kerouac typed and edited this book by William S. Burroughs and suggested its title. Critic Herbert Gold, writing in the New York Times *called* Naked Lunch *"ooty brought back from a nightmare." A couple of stanzas from a whimsical poem which Allen Ginsberg wrote in 1954, follows.*

Source: Allen Ginsberg, *Collected Poems, 1947-1980*, New York: HarperCollins, 1984. Quoted by Ann Charters, *The Portable Beat Reader*, New York: Viking Penguin, 1992, p. 101.

On Burrough's Work

The method must be purest meat
and no symbolic dressing,
Actual visions and actual prisons
as seen then and now.

....

A naked lunch is natural to us,
We eat reality sandwiches.
But allegories are so much lettuce.
Don't hide the madness.

Naked Lunch *was first published in France in 1959. Although the book was published in the U. S. in 1962, it was "banned in Boston" where the First Amendment was argued before the Massachusetts Supreme Court on October 8, 1965.*

Allen Ginsberg and Norman Mailer were among those who testified on the book's behalf and Grove Press eventually won its appeal.

Source: Watson, *op. cit.*, p. 284.

The case, finally decided by Justice William Brennan on March 21, 1966, marked a landmark in publishing history as it was the last literary work to be suppressed by U. S. Customs, the Federal Post Office, or a state government. As Allen Ginsberg put it, "the word had been liberated."

Burroughs' Cut-ups

William Burroughs developed a creative technique that involved random cutting or folding, then rearranging and pasting lines in juxtaposition. The method was similar to collages and abstract paintings then being produced by visual artists. Although Irish playwright Samuel Becket called it "plumbing instead of writing," Allen Ginsberg compared Burroughs' quick-cutting writing style to MTV images. In the following excerpt Burroughs explains how and why he wrote in this manner.

Source: William S. Burroughs, "The Cut-up Method of Brion Gysin." Quoted by Anne Waldman, editor, *The Beat Book; poems and fiction from the beat generation,* Boston, MA: Shambhala Publications, Inc.; New York: Random House, 1996, pp. 184-185.

In the summer of 1959 Brion Gysin painter and writer said "Writing is fifty years behind painting" and applied montage technique to words on a page. He cut newspaper articles into sections and rearranged the sections at random....

The cut-up method brings to writers the collage, which has been used by painters for fifty years. And used by the moving and still camera. In fact all street shots from movie or still camera are by the unpredictable factors of passersby and juxtaposition cut-ups. And photographers will tell you that often their best shots are accidents...writers will tell you the same. The best writing seems to be done almost by accident by writers until the cut-up method was made explicit—all writing is in fact cut-ups;.... You cannot

will spontaneity. But you can introduce the unpredic.
neous factor with a pair of scissors.

The method is simple. Here is one way to do it. Take
Like this page. Now cut down the middle and across the mɪ
You have four sections: 1 2 3 4.... Now rearrange the sectioɪ
placing sections four with section one and section two with section
three. And you have a new page. Sometimes it says much the same
thing. Sometimes something quite different—cutting up political
speeches is an interesting exercise—in any case you will find that
it says something and something quite definite. Take any poet or
writer you fancy. Here, say, or poems you have read over many
times. The words have lost meaning and life through years of rep-
etition. Now take the poem and type out selected passages. Fill a
page with excerpts. Now cut the page. You have a new poem As
many poems as you like....

Cut-ups are for everyone. Anybody can make cut-ups. It is
experimental in the sense of being something to do. Right here
write now. Not something to talk and argue about.... Cut the words
and see how they fall. Shakespeare, Rimbaud live in their words.
Cut the word lines and you will hear their voices....

Burroughs' Influence

Source: *USA Today*, David Bowie, August 4, 1997.

Burroughs' rechanneling of language and thought so permeates
these last years of the twentieth century that his essence remains.
For writers, he was both a challenge and a path. He helped melt
down the divide between our perceptions of reality and dreams.

Source: Edward H. Foster, *Understanding the Beats*, Columbia, South Carolina, University
of South Carolina Press, 1992, p. 198.

Burroughs is important to writers, particularly poets, in his dis-
section of language. Rock groups and performance artists like Patti
Smith and Laurie Anderson have been influenced by him. The

voice of Burroughs can be heard in *Sharkey's Night* in Anderson's 1984 *Mister Heartbreak* album.

The term 'Heavy Metal" comes from Burroughs' book, *The Soft Machine* (1961). In his final years, William Burroughs appeared in music videos for *Ministry* and U-2's *Last Night On Earth*. He appeared in the film *Drugstore Cowboy* (1989) and bassist/songwriter Bill Laswell got the author to read from his book *The Western Lands* for his album *Seven Souls*.

Listen to the Beat

Soon after moving to New York City, while a student at Horace Mann, Kerouac began going to Harlem's Apollo Theatre to listen to jazz. Seymour Wyse, a fellow student, introduced Jack to his favorite band, Count Basie, featuring Lester Young.

Source: Tom Clark, *Jack Kerouac*, New York: Harcourt Brace Jovanovich, 1984, p. 41.

In one article written for the Horace Mann Record in 1940, Jack defined "real jazz" as "music which has not been pre-arranged-free-for-all ad-lib. It is the outburst of passionate musicians, who pour all their energy into their instruments in the quest of soulful expression and super-improvisation...a soloist improvises around the melody of a song...in order to express himself with...originality and personality.... It gets you—right down to your shoe-tops!

"The Beginning of Bop"

Another example of Kerouac's favorite theme of jazz follows.

Source: Jack Kerouac, *Escapade*, April, 1959. Reprint: Donald Allen, editor, *Good Blonde & Others*, San Francisco, California: Grey Fox Press, 1993, pp. 126-131.

Bop began with jazz but one afternoon somewhere on a sidewalk maybe 1939, 1940, Dizzy Gillespie or Charley Parker or Thelonious Monk was walking down past a men's clothing store on 42nd Street or South Main in L. A. and from the loudspeaker they suddenly heard a wild impossible mistake in jazz that could only have been heard inside their own imaginary head, and that is a new art, Bop. The name derives from an accident, America was named after an Italian explorer and not after an Indian king, Lionel Hampton had made a record called "Hay Baba Ree Bop" and everybody yelled it and it was when Lionel would jump in the audience and whale his saxophone at everybody with sweat, claps, jumping fools in the aisles, the drummer booming and belaboring on his stage as the whole theater rocked...bop happened—the bird flew in—minds went in—...

"Hee ha ha!" laughs Charley Parker bending down to slap his ankle. He puts his alto to his mouth and says "Didn't I tell you!" —with jazz of notes...Bop is the language from America's inevitable Africa, going is sounded like gong, Africa is the name of the flue and kick beat, off to one side—the sudden squeak uninhibited that screams muffled at any moment from Dizzy Gillespie's trumpet....

....

The band of 10 PM Minton's swings into action, Bird Parker who is only 18 year old has a crew cut of Africa looks impossible has perfect eyes and composures of a king when suddenly you stop and look at him in the subway and you can't believe that bop is here to stay—that it is real.... "Blow!" said Diz, and Charley Parker came in for his solo with a squeaky innocent cry. Monk punched anguished nub fingers crawling at the keyboard to tear up foundations and guts of jazz from the big masterbox, to make Charley Parker hear his cry and sigh—to jar the orchestra into vibrations— to elicit gloom from the doom of the black piano. He stared down wild eyed at his keys like a matador at the bull's head.... Like 12 Century monks high in winter belfries of the Gothic Organ they wild eyed were listening to their own wild sound which was heralding in a new age of music that would eventually require symphonies, schools, centuries of technique, declines and falls of master-ripe styles—the Dixieland of Louis Armstrong sixteen in New Orleans.... Soon enough it would leap and fill the gay Twenties like champagne in a glass, pop! —And crawl up to the Thirties with tired Rudy Vallees lamenting what Louis had laughed in a Twenties Transoceanic Jazz....

David Amram Remembers Jack Kerouac

Often called "Renaissance Man of American Music," Amram has composed over one hundred orchestral and chamber works, several operas and ballets, as well as musical scores for such films as "The Manchurian Candidate" and "Splendor In the Grass." He plays French horn, piano, guitar, numerous flutes and whistles, percussion and instruments from twenty-five different countries. He continues to travel the world, composing, conducting symphony orchestras, and performing music of many cultures. In the following selection, David Amram recalls his friendship and performances with Kerouac.

Source: David Amram, October 24, 1969; reprinted with the author's permission. Printed as Kerouac obituary in January 1970 *Evergreen Review*. Full text available on David Amram's website: http://www.fmp.com/amram.

I used to see Jack often at the old Five Spot when I was working there. I knew he was a writer, and all musicians knew that he loved music. You could tell by the way he sat and listened. He never tried to seem hip. He was too interested in life around him to ever think of how he appeared. Musicians understood this and were

David Amram plays at the Five Spot club in New York in 1957.
(Burt Glinn/Magnum Photos, NY)

41

always glad to see him, because we knew that meant at least one person would be listening. Jack was on the same wave-length as we were, so it was never necessary to talk.

A few months later, poets Howard Hart and Philip Lamantia came by my place with Jack. They had decided to read their poetry with music, and Jack said he would join in, reading, improvising, rapping with the audience and singing along. Our first performance was in December of 1957 at the Brata Art Gallery on East 10th Street. It was the first jazz-poetry reading in New York. There was no advertising and it was raining, but the place was packed. Jack had become the most important figure of the time. His name was magic. In spite of the carping, whining put-downs by the furious critics, and the jealousy of some of his contemporaries for his overnight success (he had written ten books in addition to *On The Road* with almost no recognition), Jack hadn't changed. But people's reaction to him was sometimes frightening. He was suddenly being billed as the "King of The Beatniks," and manufactured against his will, as some kind of public Guru for a movement that never existed. Jack was a private person, extremely shy, and dedicated to writing. When he drank, he became much more expansive, and this was the only part of his personality that became publicized. The people who came to the Brata Gallery weren't taste makers; they were friends.

A few months later, we began some readings at the Circle in the Square. Everyone improvised, including the light man, who had his first chance to wail on the light board. The audience joined in, heckling, requesting Jack to read parts of *On The Road*, and asking him to expound on anything that came into his head. He also would sing while I was playing the horn, sometimes making up verses. He had a phenomenal ear. It was like playing duets with a great musician.

Jack was proud of his knowledge of music and of the musicians of his time. He used to come by and play the piano by ear for hours. He had some wonderful ideas for combining the spoken word with music. A few weeks later, jazz-poetry became "Official Entertainment," and a few months later was discarded as another bit of refuse, added to the huge mound of our junk culture. It was harder to dispose of Jack. The same journalists and radio and TV personalities who had heralded him were now ripping him to shreds. Fortunately, they couldn't rip up his manuscripts. His work was being published, more widely read, and translated.

In early 1958, all of us went to Brooklyn College, where Jack, Phillip and Howard read. Jack spent most of the time answering the students' questions with questions of his own. He was the down-home Zen master, and the students finally realized he wasn't putting them on. He was showing them himself. If they wanted to meet the Author Jack Kerouac, they would have to read his books....

In the spring of 1959, the film *Pull My Daisy* was made. Allen Ginsberg, Gregory Corso, Peter Orlovsky, Larry Rivers and myself...appeared in it. Alfred Leslie directed it and Robert Frank filmed it. Jack had written the scenario, and after the film had been edited, Jack saw it. Because it was a silent movie, Jack was to narrate it, and I was to write the music afterwards. He, Allen, and Neal Cassady also wrote the lyrics for the title song, for which I wrote the music, sung in the film by Anita Ellis. Jack put on earphones and asked me to play, so that he could improvise the narration to music, the way we had done at our readings. He watched the film, and made up the narration on the spot. He did it two times through spontaneously, and that was it. He refused to do it again. He believed in spontaneity, and the narration turned out to be the very best thing about the film....

In the early sixties I used to see Jack when he would come in from Northport. Once, he called up at one in the morning and told me I had to come over so that he could tell me a story. I brought over some music to copy, and Jack spoke non-stop until 8:30 a. m., describing a trip he had made through North Africa and Europe. It was like hearing a whole book of his being read aloud, and Jack was the best reader of his own work, with the exception of Dylan Thomas, that I ever heard.

"That's a fantastic story," I told him. "It sounds just like your books."

"I try to make my writing sound just the way I talk," he said. His ideal was not to display his literary skill, but to have a conversation with the reader....

Sometimes Jack would call from different parts of the country just to talk, and we continued to write to each other. In one letter he said "Ug-g-h. Fame is such a drag." He wanted time to work, but found that success robbed him of his freedom. At the same time, he felt that he was forgotten. I told him that all the young people I met when I toured colleges loved his books. To many, he was their favorite writer. But writer meant something different now. It was what was being said, not how it was said. It was content that counted, not style. Jack's message was a whole way of being, and he was becoming more an influence than ever.

Truman Capote dismissed Jack's work as "typing." I never heard Jack put down another writer. He went out of his way to encourage young writers. His work reflects this spirit of generosity, kindness and love. This is why his "typing" is so meaningful to young people today. Jack was ahead of his time spiritually. Like Charlie Parker, Lenny Bruce and Lord Buckley, his work is constantly being rediscovered....

Amram wrote the following tribute for the 25th anniversary of the publication of On The Road.

Source: Words and Music by David Amram, copyright, New Chamber Music, Inc., BMI 1994. Reprinted with author's permission.

This Song's for You, Jack

As long as there's a tree
a flower
a river
or a stream

As long as there's a swallow
a catfish
a storm cloud
and a dream

As long as there is summer rain
and early morning dew
This song's for you Jack,
This song is for you.

All the times you talked of Texas
as the sun set in the West
across New Jersey skyline
those stories were the best.

People from all over
we got to know through you
cross the Rockies, down to Mexico
far from New York Sixth Avenue

two floors up, one room, scat-singing
laughing dancing poetry all night through
the good times and rivers roll along
so I wrote this song for you.

Moon light bright October night
in Lowell, Massachusetts
birds fly South
on their winter way

Casting moon-lit shadows
on the road
you traveled
yesterday

The wind blows East
from Denver
in San Francisco
clouds are turning gray.

You stayed and left
a thousand places
searching for Bhudda
Brittany and Spain

Walked through Colorado holly
heard the ancient South Dakota drum
of Sitting Bull
drank Oklahoma rain

You wrote us stories
by your brakeman's shining lantern
through the night on rusty tracks in Texas
on the roadsie by the train

The road
you shared with us
the road you showed us
we can ride on too

We share the ride
you're by our side
Jack this song's
for you.

(Audience sings)
This song's for you Jack,
This song's for you.

This song's for you Jack,
This song's for you.

Together on the road tonight
we share the holy highway light
This song's for you Jack,
This song's for you.

Perhaps because English was his second language, Kerouac had a special ear for sounds which are as significant throughout his work as visual metaphor. He frequently read into a tape recorder to hear what he had written on paper and was determined to write in the same way that a jazz musician blows choruses of invention on an instrument, from his head. He called this "Bop Prosody."

Source: Jack Kerouac, *Mexico City Blues* (242 Choruses), New York: Grove Press, 1959, p. 241.

NOTE

I want to be considered a jazz poet
blowing a long blues in an afternoon jam
session on Sunday. I take 242 choruses;
my ideas vary and sometimes roll from
chorus to chorus or from halfway through
a chorus to halfway into the next.

Gregory Corso
(1930-   )

"Street Urchin Shelley"

Abandoned by his teenage mother six months after his birth in New York's Greenwich Village, Corso spent his childhood being passed from his father to foster homes. At the age of twelve, he was sent to reform school for stealing a radio, where he suffered physical abuse. Later he lived on the streets, sleeping in subways and on rooftops. He began to write poetry and study great literature, particularly the English poet, Shelley, in state prison, where he was incarcerated from age sixteen to nineteen. Corso met Ginsberg in New York City in 1950, who introduced him to Kerouac and other friends, encouraged him to continue writing and later became his literary agent.

Source: Jack Kerouac for cover of *Gasoline* by Gregory Corso. San Francisco, California: City Lights, 1955, 1958.

I think that Gregory Corso and Allen Ginsberg are the two best poets in America and that they can't be compared to each other. Gregory was a tough young kid from the Lower East Side who rose like an angel over the rooftops and sang Italian songs as sweet as Caruso and Sinatra, but in words. "Sweet Milanese hills" brood in his Renaissance soul, evening is coming on the hills. Amazing and beautiful Gregory Corso, the one and only Gregory The Herald....

Corso is admired for his poetic wit. The problem he has always had making decisions is a recurring theme through his work. "If you have a choice of two things & can't decide, take both!" Following are some excerpts from the poem, "Marraige."

Source: Gregory Corso, Excerpt from "Marriage," *The Happy Birthday of Death*, New York: New Directions Publishing Corp., 1960. (Reprinted by permission of New Directions Publishing Corp.)

Marriage

Should I get married? Should I be good?
Astound the girl next door with my velvet suit
     and faustus hood?
Don't take her to movies but to cemeteries
tell all about werewolf bathtubs and forked clarinets
then desire her and kiss her and all the preliminaries
and she going just so far and I understanding why

....

When she introduces me to her parents
back straightened, hair finally combed, strangled by
     a tie.
should I sit knees together on their 3rd degree sofa
and not ask Where's the bathroom?
How else to feel other than I am,
often thinking Flash Gordon soap—
O how terrible it must be for a young man
seated before a family and the family thinking
We never saw him before! He wants our Mary Lou!
After tea and homemade cookies they ask What do you
     do for a living?
Should I tell them? Would they like me then?
Say All right get married, we're losing a daughter
but we're gaining a son—

....

O God, and the wedding! All her family and her friends
and only a handful of mine all scroungy and bearded
just wait to get at the drinks and food—

....

Then all that absurd rice and clanky cans and shoes
Niagra Falls! Hordes of us! Husbands! Wives!
     Flowers! Chocolates!

....

But I should get married I should be good
How nice it'd be to come home to her
and sit by the fireplace and she in the kitchen
aproned young and lovely wanting my baby
and so happy about me she burns the roast beef
and comes crying to me and I get up from my big
       papa chair...

Yet if I should get married and it's Connecticut and
       snow
and she gives birth to a child and I am sleepless, worn,
up for nights, head bowed against a quiet window, the
       past behind me,
finding myself in the most common of situations
       a trembling man
knowledged with responsibility and not twig-smear nor
       Roman coin soup—
O what would that be like!
Surely I'd give it for a nipple a rubber Tacitus
For a rattle a bag of broken Bach records
Tack Della Francesca all over its crib
Sew the Greek alphabet on its bib
And build for its playpen a roofless Parthenon

No, I doubt I'd be that kind of father
not rural not snow no quiet window
but hot smelly tight New York City
seven flights up, roaches and rats in the walls
a fat Reichian wife screeched over potatoes Get a job!
And five nose running brats in love with Batman
And the neighbors all toothless and dry haired
like those hag masses of the 18th century
all wanting to come in and watch TV
The landlord wants his rent

Grocery store Blue Cross Gas & Electric Knights of
       Columbus
Impossible to lie back and dream Telephone snow,
       ghost parking—
No! I should not get married I should never get
       married!
But —imagine If I were married to a beautiful
       sophisticated woman
tall and pale wearing an elegant black dress and long
       black gloves
holding a cigarette holder in one hand and highball in
       the other
and we live high up a penthouse with a huge window
from which we could see all of New York and even
       farther on clearer days
No, can't imagine myself married to that pleasant prison
       dream

O but what about love? I forget love
not that I am incapable of love
it's just that I see love as odd as wearing shoes—
I never wanted to marry a girl who was like my mother
And Ingrid Bergman was always impossible
And there's maybe a girl now but she's already married
And I don't like men and—
but there's got to be somebody!
Because what if I'm 60 years old and not married?…

Lawrence Ferlinghetti
(1919-   )

Born to immigrant parents in Yonkers, New York, Ferlinghetti received his BA from the University of North Carolina and served as a naval Lieutenant Commander during World War II. In 1947, he returned to graduate school on the G. I. Bill, receiving a Master's in literature from Columbia and a Ph.D from the Sorbonne in Paris. He moved to San Francisco, where he co-founded City Lights, America's first paperback bookstore.

Bob Donlon, Neal Cassady, Allen Ginsberg, Robert La Vigne, and Lawrence Ferlinghetti outside of City Lights Bookstore, 1956. Photo by Allen Ginsberg

Named in honor of Charlie Chaplin's film, and located in North Beach, City Lights became a center for the San Francisco Renaissance. An accomplished poet, novelist, playwright, and painter, Ferlinghetti continues to write and to publish works by avant guarde writers. Following is an brief excerpt from one of his more whimsical poems.

Source: Lawrence Ferlinghetti, *A Coney Island of the Mind*, New York: New Directions, 1958, pp. 67-68. (Reprinted by permission of New Directions Publishing Corp.)

Dog

The dog trots freely in the street
and sees reality
and the things he sees
are bigger than himself
and the things he sees
are his reality
Drunks in doorways
Moons on trees
The dog trots freely thru the street
and the things he sees
are smaller than himself
Fish on newsprint
Ants in holes
Chickens in Chinatown windows
their heads a block away
The dog trots freely in the street
and the things he smells
smell something like himself
The dog trots freely in the street
past puddles and babies
cats and cigars
poolrooms and policemen
He doesn't hate cops
He merely has no use for them
and he goes past them
and past the dead cows hung up whole
in front of the San Francisco Meat Market
He would rather eat a tender cow
than a tough policeman
though either might do
And he goes past the Romeo Ravioli Factory
and past Coit's Tower

and past Congressman Doyle
He's afraid of Coit's Tower
but he's not afraid of Congressman Doyle
although what he hears is very discouraging
very depressing
very absurd
to a sad young dog like himself
to a serious dog like himself
But he has his own free world to live in
His own fleas to eat
He will not be muzzled
Congressman Doyle is just another
fire hydrant
to him
the dog trots freely in the street
and has his own dog's life to live
and to think about
and to reflect upon
touching and tasting and testing everything
investigating everything
without benefit of perjury
a real realist
with a real tale to tell
and a real tail to tell it with
a real live
      barking
            democratic dog
engaged in real
      free enterprise
with something to say
      about ontology
something to say
      about reality
            and how to see it
                 and how to hear it....

Gary Snyder
(1930-   )

"Rucksack Revolution"

Two weeks after the Six Gallery reading, Kerouac and Snyder went on the mountain-climbing trip that would be retold in The Dharma Bums, *in which Snyder, as protagonist "Japhy Ryder," became "number one Dharma Bum of them all."*

Gary Snyder as "Japhy Ryder" envisions a "Rucksack Revolution," with the "Dharma Bums."

Source: Jack Kerouac, *The Dharma Bums*, New York: Penguin Books, 1958, pp. 9-10.

...refusing to subscribe to the general demand that they consume production of things they didn't really want such as refrigerators, TV sets, cars, at least new, fancy cars, certain hair oils, and deodorants, and general junk you finally always see a week later in the garbage anyway, all of them imprisoned in a system of work, produce, consume, work, produce, consume, I see a vision of a great rucksack revolution, thousands or even millions of young Americans wandering around with rucksacks, going up to mountains to pray, making children laugh and old men glad, making young girls happy and old girls happier, all of 'em Zen Lunatics who go about writing poems that happen to appear in their heads for no reason and also by being kind and also by strange, unexpected acts keep giving visions of eternal freedom to everybody and to all living creatures.

Although Gary Snyder, attended the Six Gallery reading and was identified with the Beats in his '20s, as part of the San Francisco Renaissance, he has followed his own path. After graduating from Reed College, he pursued graduate studies at Berkeley in Oriental languages, then lived in Japan, studying under Buddhist monks. In tune with the natural world through Buddhism, he has become increasingly active in the ecological movement, speaking for the environment through poetry. He received the Pulitzer Prize for Poetry in 1975. In the following excerpts, Snyder explains how his Buddhism and identification with nature continue to influence his work.

Source: David Kherdian, *Six San Francisco Poets*, Fresno: California, 1969, p. 35, p. 26.

Through Zen, the poet faces in two directions: one is to the world of people and language and society, and the other is to the non human, non verbal world, which is nature as nature in itself; and the world of human nature—the inner world—as it is itself, before language, before custom, before culture. There's no words in that world. There aren't any rules that we know and that's the area that Buddhism studies.

I try to hold both history and wilderness in mind, that my poems may approach the true measure of things and stand against the unbalance and ignorance of our times.

The following poem was inspired by Snyder's jobs as a forest ranger and his wilderness experiences.

Source: Anne Waldman, editor, *The Beat Book: poems and fiction from the beat generation*, Boston, MA: Shambhala Publications, Inc., New York: Random House, 1996. p. 289.

Mid-August At Sourdough Mountain Lookout

Down valley a smoke haze
Three days heat, after five days rain
Pitch glows on the fir-cones
Across rocks and meadows
Swarms of new flies.

I cannot remember things I once read
A few friends, but they are in cities.
Drinking cold snow-water from a tin cup
Looking down for miles
Through high still air.

Raised in the Jewish faith, Allen Ginsberg became a dedicated Buddhist under the influence of Gary Snyder as well as studies with gurus in India, China, and Tibet. The poet's sense of humor is evident in the following excerpt in which he instructs readers in the Buddhist practice of meditation.

Source: Allen Ginsberg, *Selected Poems 1947-1995*, New York: HarperCollins, Inc., 1996. (Allen Ginsberg Trust)

Do the Meditation Rock

If you want to learn   how to meditate
I'll tell you now   cause it's never too late
I'll tell you how   cause I can't wait
it's just that great   that it's never too late

....

The first thing you do   when you meditate
is keep your spine   your backbone straight
Sit yourself down   on a pillow on the ground
or sit in a chair   if the ground isn't there

Do the meditation   *Do the meditation*
　　Learn a little Patience and Generosity

Follow your breath out   open your eyes
and sit there steady   & sit there wise
Follow your breath right   outta your nose
follow it out   as far as it goes...

Do the meditation   *Do the meditation....*
　　Generosity Generosity Generosity & Generosity

Joyce Johnson

"A Minor Character"

Young women faced new options in the fifties, questioning their family-life, values, and sexuality. Joyce Johnson spent her late teens and early twenties in New York, before discovering Jack Kerouac, with whom she would have an affair.

Source: Joyce Johnson, "Leaving Home in the 1950s," from *America Firsthand*, Vol. II, New York: St. Martin's Press, 1983, pp. 252-253. (Reprinted with permission of Joyce Johnson.)

The Sunday the article on Allen [Ginsberg, the "Beat" poet] appeared, Elise called and read it to me over the phone, her voice taut with excitement. With that, our collective travel fantasies switched over to San Francisco, city of poets and accessible by Greyhound bus, whose hilly streets in our imaginations took on a pelpetual golden haze. I thought about San Francisco the way I'd thought about the Village when I was thirteen, before I ever went there. Could it possibly be what it was said to be? A vision of community into which I would somehow fit. I didn't seem to fit into the rest of America, although I did it better than Elise. It took great effort and vigilance to report to my job on Madison Avenue, my hair wound into a chignon around a horrible doughnut-shaped thing called a rat. My office identity seemed as precarious as my hair style. Someday they would find me out. I had broken the law, I had slept with men, I had contempt for the books the MCA Literary Agency was attempting to sell to publishers. The lives of my superiors seemed desiccated rather than enviable. Only the publication of my novel would transform my existence into what I wanted it to be....

A Barnard friend of mine worked for *Mademoiselle*. I visited her there one day and she showed me proofs of the article they were gong to run on the San Francisco Renaissance. There was a photo of Allen with three other men, a cherubic hoodlum named Gregory Corso, a scholarly Philip Whalen, and a writer who had a crucifix around his neck and tangled black hair plastered against his forehead as if he'd just walked out of the rain. He looked wild and sad in a way that didn't seem appropriate to the occasion. This was Jack Kerouac, whose reputation was underground. Like the others, he was said to frequent North Beach, a run-down area where there were suddenly a lot of new coffee shops, jazz joints, and bars, as well as an excellent bookstore called City Lights that was the center of activity for the poets. Thus several thousand young women between fourteen and twenty-five were given a map to a revolution. *Mademoiselle* made it its business to keep up with things.

I remembered the man with the dark, anguished face and the name that was unlike anyone else's, the harsh music of its three syllables. Soon afterward I found it on a book at the office. A battered copy of *The Town and the City* was on a shelf where they put things that weren't active any more. I asked what it was doing at MCA, and was told it was the work of a talented but very terrible person who had briefly been handled by the agency. He had grown more and more enraged and unreasonable as his various novels proved impossible to place. Sometimes he seemed under the influence of alcohol—or worse, probably. Then one day an equally crazy Mr. Ginsberg had turned up without an appointment, demanding the return of the three manuscripts and announcing that he was Jack Kerouac's agent. Good riddance!

I asked if I could borrow Kerouac's book. I took it home and never brought it back.

The Beat Goes On

by
Juliet Haines Mofford

"It's our work that counts, if anything at all."

— Jack Kerouac, 1967-

Some of the early Beats became part of the sixties counterculture. Neal Cassady drove the Merry Pranksters' psychedelic bus. Allen Ginsberg became a political activist, demonstrating against the Vietnam War and nuclear testing, and in support of gay rights. Gary Snyder continues his active ecological leadership. However, the real revolution of the Beat Generation was in literature. The works of the Beat writers that so shocked the establishment in the 1950s has now become part of the fabric of our contemporary culture.

On The Road has been translated into some thirty-two languages and is internationally considered one of the great "Coming of Age" books as it is rediscovered by each new generation. Kerouac's biographer and editor, Ann Charters, ranks its significance in American literature with *Moby Dick*, *The Scarlet Letter*, and *Huckleberry Finn*.

In 1975, when Bob Dylan brought his *Rolling Thunder Revue* to Lowell, Massachusetts, he made a pilgrimage to Kerouac's grave site with Allen Ginsberg. Dylan told Ginsberg that *Mexico City Blues* was one of his favorite books and that "Kerouac was the first poet to talk to me in my own language."

Many other contemporary writers and musicians have paid homage to Kerouac in spirit and style: the Grateful Dead's Jerry Garcia, novelist Ken Kesey, poet-political activist Ed Saunders, rock star Patti Smith, and playwright-actor Sam Shepherd. 10,000 Maniacs recorded their original "Hey, Jack Kerouac." Tom Waits honored "Jack and Neal" in song and Morphine recently recorded Mark Sandman's poem "Kerouac."

Anne Waldman, performance poet and author of *Fast Speaking Woman*, among other works, founded the Jack Kerouac School of Disembodied poetics at Naropa Institute in Boulder, Colorado, with Allen Ginsberg, in 1974. It is the only accredited Buddhist college in the country.

Jack Kerouac Commemorative, Eastern Canal Park, Lowell
(Jim Higgins Photo)

The Beat writers have finally earned acceptance as serious writers. In the excerpt below, William S. Burroughs comments on the Beat Generation and its literary legacy.

Source: Ann Charters, editor, *The Portable Beat Reader*, New York: Viking Penguin, 1992, p. xxxi.

Once started, the Beat movement had a momentum of its own and a world-wide impact. In fact, the intelligent conservatives in America saw this as a serious threat to their position long before the Beat writers saw it themselves. A much more serious thereat, say, than the Communist party. The Beat literary movement came at exactly the right time and said something that millions of people of all nationalities all over the world were waiting to hear. You can't tell anybody anything he doesn't know already. The alienation, the restlessness, the dissatisfaction were already there waiting when Kerouac pointed out the road.

Artists to my mind are the real architects of change, and not political legislators, who implement change after the fact. Art exerts a profound influence on the style of life, the mode, range and direction of perception. Art tells us that we know and don't know that we know. Certainly *On the Road* performed that function in 1957 to an extraordinary extent. There's no doubt that we're living in a freer America as a result of the Beat literary cultural and political change in this country during the last forty years, when a four letter word couldn't appear on the printed page, and minority rights were ridiculous.

Suggestions for Reading, Viewing & Listening

Allen Ginsberg: "When the Muse Calls, Answer!" Tom Vitale, Host. (A Movable Feast: Profiles of Contemporary American Authors). New York: Time Arts Media, Atlas Video, 1991.

Charters, Ann. *Beats & Company: Twenty Years of Photographic Work.* (Introduction by John Clellon Holmes.) New York: Doubleday, 1986.

Gifford, Barry and Lawrence Lee. *Jack's Book: An Oral Biography.* New York: St. Martin's Press, 1978.

Halper, Jn, editor. *Gary Snyder: Dimensions of a Life.* San Francisco: Sierra Club Books, 1991.

The Jack Kerouac Collection. Santa Monica, California: word BEAT/Rhino Records, 1990.

The Jack Kerouac ROMnibus. (multimedia CD-ROM) Largely Literary/ Penguin Electronic, 1996.

Kerouac. Produced & directed by John Antonelli and Will Parrinello; narrated by Peter Coyote, 1985. (Retitled *On the Road with Jack Kerouac*, 1990).

kicks joy darkness (a spoken word tribute to Kerouac with music). Various artists. Rykodisc DC and cassette. Produced by Jim Sampas, 1997.

The Life & Times of Allen Ginsberg. Film directed by Jerry Aronson. Greenwich Village, New York: First Run Features, 1994.

Lowell Celebrates Kerouac, Inc., P. O. Box 1111, Lowell, MA 01853: annual festival, literary contest, tours and special programs.

Miles, Barry. *Ginsberg: A Biography.* New York: Simon and Schuster, 1989.

Schumacher, Michael. *Dharma Lion: A Biography of Allen Ginsberg.* New York: St. Martin's Press, 1992.

Silesky, Barry. *Ferlinghetti: The Artist In His Time.* New York: Warner Books, 1990.

Tytell, John. *Naked Angels: The Lives & Literature of the Beat Generation.* New York: McGraw-Hill, 1976. (Second edition, Grove Press, 1991.)

About the Editor

Juliet Mofford holds degrees from Tufts University and Boston University. She has taught American literature and history in Japan, Puerto Rico, and Spain. She worked as a youth services and reference librarian before becoming a full-time museum educator. A free-lance writer for thirty years, two books she wrote on New England history received citations from the American Association of State & Local History. She currently serves as a consultant for Museum Education Services, Inc., developing museum-to-schools curricula and researching primary sources to script dramatic programs for historical societies. This is the fourth book she had edited for the *Perspectives on History Series*.

During the seven years Mofford worked for the Lowell Historical Preservation Commission, she served on the Lowell Celebrates Kerouac Committee, planning annual festivals and overseeing literary contests. She had the opportunity of hosting Allen Ginsberg, Michael McClure, David Amram, Gregory Corso, Robert Creeley, Ann Charters, and others included in "The Beat Generation." Mofford has been enthusiastic about Beat literature since discovering Kerouac in college. She claims that Lawrence Ferlinghetti's poems from *A Coney Island of the Mind*, beginning "I am waiting for a rebirth of wonder," and "Let's go," inspired her family to make major life-changes a number of times. While preparing this book, she retraced the steps of her subjects in San Francisco, visiting City Lights Bookstore and other North Beach haunts.